Look, Stop Hiding!

How to Find Your Voice and
Never Dim Your Light Again!

Dr. Kristen Guillory

Look, Stop Hiding! How to Find Your Voice and Never Dim Your Light Again!

Copyright © 2021 Dr. Kristen Guillory

All rights reserved.

No part of this book may be reproduced or transmitted in any form or by any means without written permission from the author.

ISBN: 978-1-954595-05-7

Library of Congress Control Number: 2021911526

Editor: Sharp Editorial

Sparkle Publishing
www.sparklepublishing.net

Printed in the USA.

Duncanville, Texas

Dedication

This book is dedicated to my grandmother, Mimi, who showed me how to use my voice unapologetically.

Table of Contents

Introduction 1

Your Story Matters 9

Look! No More Dimming Your Light 23

Breaking Out of the Box 35

Their Understanding Is NOT Required… Okay? 51

Over It! 61

Time to Dream 69

Paralyzing Thoughts 79

Yaaas! You Better Show Up 89

It's Time to Shine and Find Your Voice 97

I Recognize! 103

The Dangers of Not Letting Your Light Shine 109

41 Not-So-Typical Speaker Tips 115

Introduction

It was my first semester of graduate school. I was working on a master's in social work (shout out to everyone with social work degrees!) During the Foundations of Social Work course, we were given topics for our final presentation. My topic was settlement houses. Settlement houses were created to provide resources to urban, poor, and immigrant European women.

When presentation day arrived, I walked to the front of the classroom, faced my classmates, and said in a very matter-of-fact tone:

So, when I first got the topic of settlement houses, I really was not interested in doing this because when I started to research settlement houses, I discovered that they did not provide anything for my ancestors. The settlement houses were specifically for immigrants from Europe. So, I began to think, "What is this doing for Black people? This program wouldn't have helped any of my people." As I continued to research, I discovered that Jane Addams, a prominent figure in social work who founded the Chicago Hull House (settlement house), was one of the founders of the NAACP, which made me more interested in my assigned topic.

After my opening, I continued to share information about settlement houses, Jane Addams, and social work. I received a nice round of applause at the end. After class, one of my classmates said, "Oh my gosh! That was so good. You are such a good speaker. How did you do that?"

I remember thinking, "What are you talking about? I was just being me."

In another social work course during another semester, we received peer feedback a week after giving our presentations. My feedback read:

You have a great presenting voice.

Great use of humor.

Great personality.

Way to break out of the box.

Another statement read, "Great humor but too much flavor."

Wow!

Too much flavor?

Introduction

Truth be told, I never saw that statement until many years later. I'm kind of glad I didn't, either.

Later, when defending my dissertation, I included photographs of young men in my presentation. Generally, pictures and personalization are not included in dissertation defenses. Frankly, most defenses are boring, and I wanted to highlight the essence of my research and flavor. My dissertation was titled *Assessment of Social Support and Peer Influence as Factors Contributing to High School Completion Among African American Males.*

I included a picture of a young man I had known and a picture of two men who completed my research surveys. Here is the thing about that – these men requested to be in the presentation. They said, "If we do this, you have to put our pictures in your presentation."

I shared that fun fact in my dissertation defense. When I concluded my presentation, I went to the hall. I was brought back in five minutes later and conferred as Dr. Kristen Guillory! My dissertation committee began to give feedback. One of my committee members said, "You should really consider public speaking and present this at an academic conference."

I did not think I had done anything that extraordinary but include two pictures of people I know.

I had no clue that being exactly who I am was enough. In fact, being myself was more than enough. People saw gifts and talents in me way before I ever did.

What about you?

Have others seen your gifts before you?

Have you struggled with knowing that you are enough just as you are?

Although I was comfortable displaying my personality and flavor, that faded for a while as I spent many years dimming my light. *But no more!*

I wonder if you have hidden who you really are or tried to fit into a mold. Have you ever dimmed your light? If so, you are in the right place.

I have had the honor to be a professor, therapist, director of programs of a social work agency, and public speaker. I have spoken over 1,000 times to over 100,000 people. I have often been the only woman, person of color, and Black person invited to share at these events. I had to realize that it was important to show up fully as myself. I had to realize that my voice and story matter. I had to realize that not everyone will like me. So, they might as well not like the real me because trying to be someone else is exhausting.

In January of 2018, the Lord gave me the idea to create a speaker bootcamp. I hosted the first camp in April of 2018 and earned my first one-on-one speaker client in May of 2018, and as they say, the rest is history. I have been honored to coach hundreds of phenomenal people and lead quite a few public speaking trainings reaching thousands of people around the world. While I love being a speaker coach, I never thought I would be doing what I am doing. Still, I know that everything I have experienced professionally and personally contributes to my ability to support my clients. About 98% of my clients are Black, and 90% are women. When I get the chance to support these brilliant men and women, two common elements always arise:

1. These people hide who they are, hide their personalities, their gifts, and their voices.
2. These people dim their light.

I did not realize, as a speaker coach, that I would use my gift of the ability to help people heal. Helping my clients is so much more than getting them on stage. It is helping them to walk in the freedom of who they are, which is healing. It is helping them to know they do not have to try to fit into certain boxes. It is helping them to see their value.

Clients have told me that their word to describe how they feel after working with me is *freedom*. They have shared that I give them permission and freedom to be exactly who they are. One client even described me as the Harriet Tubman of speaking because I set their voices free.

I had another client that supports those in the military transitioning to civilian life. While working on a workshop for this group, he included a story about waiting to get the news about whether a certain company would hire him. I encouraged him to add details describing how he felt waiting on the news. He shared that he was "skurred."

"I need you to say that," I told him. "And then how did you feel when you learned that you didn't get the job?" I asked.

He said, "I wanted to say 'damn, damn, damn" like Florida Evans from *Good Times*. Can I say that?" he asked.

"Absolutely," I replied.

About one month later, he led this workshop with his new additions. After, he told me he had been leading trainings and workshops for years but got the best feedback and response he ever received after that workshop. He thanked me and was grateful for my guidance in helping him show up as his authentic self not only on that stage but in all aspects of his life.

And look! I want to help you, too! If you ever dimmed your light, not believed who you are is enough, code switched, dealt with imposter syndrome, or hid who you are, this book is for you.

How to prepare for this book

This book is for you if you desire to no longer hide, want to walk in the freedom of who you are, or rediscover your voice. As a bonus, there are 41 not-so-typical public speaking tips included. I encourage you to spend time at the end of each chapter answering the questions and rereading the sections you need. Get your journal and pen ready. We have work to do. And as I like to say, do not ever dim your light again. If it is too bright, they can put on sunglasses. Now look, it's time to find your voice and never dim your light again!

Let's shine!

Your Story Matters

I was 25 years old and tutoring a teacher at Carter High School in Dallas, Texas. This teacher was in graduate school, and I was helping her with statistics coursework. One day, she said, "You're in school, right? What are you working on?"

"Yes, I'm in school. I'm working on my Ph.D.," I replied.

"Oh, my goodness!" she exclaimed. "How old are you?"

"I'm 25," I answered.

"Oh, my goodness," she said again. "Would you be willing to talk to my students? They need to see someone like you."

"Sure!" I agreed.

As we continued to chat, another teacher walked into the room and said, "Hey! What's going on?"

The teacher I was tutoring said, "This is Kristen. She is 25 years old, working on a Ph.D., and she is helping me with my coursework. And she's going to speak to my students!"

The other teacher marveled and asked if I would speak to her students, too, to which I agreed.

In a matter of ten minutes, I was invited to speak to about 300 students.

I was excited and nervous. I knew I would put together the most amazing presentation. I was truly honored to be invited.

That night, I went to the Wednesday night service at church. During praise and worship, I heard the Lord give me ideas for my presentation.

I love praise and worship, but I had to sit and jot down all the ideas He gave me.

My mind was made up. I would talk about people I knew that had overcome something.

The next day, I emailed 14 friends from high school and college and asked them if they would be interested in being a part of this amazing opportunity. I told them I would include them in the presentation. I asked for a picture and brief details about what they overcame.

To my pleasant surprise, every person emailed me back and agreed to be a part of my presentation. Every person!

I spent the next two weeks working on my presentation. I implemented all the fancy PowerPoint tricks available in 2006. Yes, all of them! I downloaded 15 different instrumentals from the most popular hip hop and R&B songs for the presentation, embedded them, and used slide transitions. I titled the presentation "Houston, We Have a Problem," which was also the title of a song by my brother-in-law, and that song was the 15th song of my presentation. I knew I was putting together the most amazing presentation.

Well, two weeks had passed, and the time had come to present.

It was the end of the school year in 2006. I walked on campus feeling excited and nervous. I would be speaking to 12 different classes within two days. I was ready!

I walked into the classroom of the teacher I was tutoring. I began to set up. I hooked up my laptop to the projector and made sure the sound and screen were working.

Look, Stop Hiding!

It was showtime.

As the students walked in, I began to play the song "Houston, We Have a Problem" by Tedashii. As soon as they heard the music, they immediately smiled and gave me "the nod." This told me that I made the right choice to play music. I became even more excited. My adrenaline was pumping.

The teacher introduced me, and I began going through the slides with music. Everything was perfect! I was showing pictures of my high school classmates and telling their powerful stories. The students were engaged. They were asking questions. They were bobbing their heads to the music. I even invited a few students to freestyle, aka rap. Ayyyyeee!

Apparently, after that presentation, word got around about me.

Later that day, another staff member was interested in me presenting at another time, but I was unable to accept that invitation.

The next day, I returned to do it all over again. It was going well once again. The students and teachers loved it. I loved it! The students did not want to leave. I could not believe the amazing time I had speaking to over 300 students in two days. This presentation would become one of my most popular presentations during my first two years of speaking. I would go on to present "Houston, We Have a Problem" at least 20 times over the next two years.

About six months after speaking at Carter High School, I was invited by my alma mater, Texas Christian University (Go Frogs!), to speak to a group of students. I was excited! During the call to discuss the event, I was asked if I could tell my story and talk about my experience on campus as a Black student.

My first thought was, "I don't really have a story that would be appealing. I don't have any grand moments to share." I even considered bringing a friend with me, a fellow TCU graduate and NFL player. When I told my dad about this plan, he said, "Kristen, no, they invited you." And he was right.

Each of us is unique and has something special to offer. Comparing our experiences can diminish our voices and lead us to believe that other stories are better and more impactful. At the time, that is exactly what I thought. I was beginning to learn that I did not have to compromise or dismiss my voice. So, I did not invite my friend. I went, just me, and I gave a talk about… me.

It was strange, very strange for me to talk about…me. The talk was okay. My mom, aunt, and three girls I mentored were there and said, "Yeah, it was good, but you seemed nervous."

I *was* nervous. But I was more uncomfortable.

I was not used to talking about myself.

I didn't think I had anything to offer. I thought other people's stories were better than mine.

Three months after that uncomfortable speaking engagement, another university contacted me. One of the sororities was hosting a large event for the women on campus, and they wanted me to be their keynote speaker.

Whaaaat?! Me? The keynote speaker? I was honored.

I thought back to my Carter High School speaking engagement. While it was so fun and the students enjoyed it, as I was prepping for my keynote talk, I realized that I did not talk about myself. I shared about my friends and their amazing stories, but essentially, I left myself out.

Why?

I did not think my story was powerful. I did not think my story had the elements of a moving story. I did not consider the reason I was invited to speak to the students. The teachers were impressed that a 25-year-old Black woman was working on a Ph.D., and they wanted their students to meet me. I did not consider that being who I was and doing what I was doing was impressive and enough.

As I began to prepare for this keynote engagement, I decided to do something different. I decided that this was the moment I would be me. I was going to share me. I was going to show the true me. My story did not have elements that I thought would typically be in a powerful story, but nevertheless, it was my story. I wanted to honor my journey. I was discovering that my journey and story were powerful. I decided to title this "Talk PG-6."

Why?

I shared about being in my high school band (shout out to the clarinets!) I shared about being in Advanced Placement (AP) courses and having self-esteem issues. I shared about the peer pressure I experienced in college from some of my girlfriends who encouraged me to do things with guys I did not want to do. I talked about being a virgin and believing in abstinence. I talked about entering graduate school on academic probation and earning a 4.0 the first semester. I shared about having a dean who was a hater when I was working on my Ph.D. This dean had told me I would not graduate with my Ph.D. because I was young and single. I was also the only Black person in my cohort. I then told the women in the audience that I did the motorcycle dance from the song "It's Going Down" by Yung Joc during my Ph.D. graduation.

My audience was captivated. They were on that journey with me. They laughed during the funny parts, danced when I referenced music, and clapped and cheered. That was one of the first moments of speaking at an event when I felt like I was being me.

To my surprise, within 48 hours, I received more than ten emails from women in the audience. These women expressed their appreciation for me being there.

Although this took place in 2008, I remember some of those messages in detail. In one of the messages, one of the women revealed that her stepfather and stepbrother had abused her. In another message, one of the women said she had considered suicide. In another message, a woman shared her past abuse. As I read those emails, I was overwhelmed with gratitude for the thank yous and appreciation notes, but I was also a bit confused about why some of these women shared very personal things with me. I remember thinking, "But I didn't mention anything about abuse or suicide."

The next day, I sat back and understood why they shared with me. It's not that we had the same story. It was that I had a story and shared it with transparency. I was vulnerable and shared some challenges I experienced. At that moment, I truly recognized that my story is powerful, and transparency and vulnerability are extremely important.

Look, Stop Hiding!

Describe something you have shared that impressed others, yet you did not think it was a big deal.

_____

_____

_____

Why did others think it was a big deal?

_____

_____

_____

To Do

What are three challenges you have overcome?

1. _____
2. _____
3. _____

What are three of your achievements?

1. _____
2. _____
3. _____

What are three of your gifts or strengths?

1. _____
2. _____
3. _____

What are three things other people say you do well?

1. _____
2. _____
3. _____

What parts of your story and journey have you underestimated?

_____

_____

_____

_____

What parts of your story and journey are big deals?

_____

_____

_____

_____

Do you know how many makeup lines, car brands, and types of bread are out there? Regardless of the number, there are plenty of people who believe those brands are all special. Well, there is only one you, only one person with your exact experiences. You are special. Why have you ever thought your story and journey are not enough?

_____

_____

_____

_____

List three reasons your story is enough. (Feel free to include comments from your friends.)

1. _____
2. _____
3. _____

Look! No More Dimming Your Light

I had on my red dress, thick gold belt, cute jean blazer, and high heels. I knew I wanted to be so fresh and so clean.

It was the first day of the first semester of my first full-time professor position. I was excited and had first-day jitters. I decided to do a little something different during the first class. Instead of doing the typical thing where class starts with everyone introducing themselves and then reviewing the syllabus for the remaining time, I decided to play my theme song, "Never Find Another." This is a hip-hop song that was created by a young man I mentored and his friend. As the song played, I danced a bit and had the students snap their fingers with me. The class really enjoyed the music.

Fast forward to the next semester.

It was day one, and I began with my welcome presentation. I was about 20 minutes into the class lecture when one of the students raised her hand and said, "Wait a minute, Dr. Guillory. Where is your song?"

I was surprised by her question.

I asked, "What are you talking about?

She said, "Where is your theme song?"

"How do you even know about that song?" I had asked.

She said, "That's what everybody was talking about last semester. They were talking about your music and you as a new, young, Black professor."

"Look, y'all," I said. "I'm already one of the youngest professors here. No one is playing a hip-hop theme song."

I was thinking about the fact that I was one of the only Black women professors, and I did not want to stand out too much. I was also worried about the stereotype threat. Although I played it during the first semester, I allowed those limiting thoughts and beliefs to get the best of me.

The students said, "So! That is what everybody mentioned about you. That is what they loved about you.

"Okay," I said. "My theme song it is!" I played the song, and we jammed together as a class.

That was a significant moment for me never to dim my light again. Unfortunately, that would not be the last time I would do so.

Years into my speaking career, I became aware that not everyone was always excited to see me. I learned that some folks did not want me to attend some of the events because they thought I would "beat" them, be the best, or take the attention away from them. Due to this, there were moments I considered toning myself down.

There were times I tried to dim my blessing of being single because some find it weird to see someone so happy, content, *and* single. And yes, being single is a blessing if one allows it to be.

While in my early 20s, I often pretended to want to talk about men and dating because those were the go-to conversation topics. Because I did not know how to communicate that I did not want those to be the only topics of conversation, I stopped attending certain outings.

When I began as a professor, I did not want anyone to know I was in my 20s. I thought they wouldn't take me seriously. I am the only person I know who was excited about turning 30.

I had women tell me not to mention my credentials because men would not want me.

Nah, I did not follow that encouragement.

I remember being at the beauty salon. I showed some of the ladies my new business cards, which were the size of a postcard. I had one of my new professional pictures on one side, and on the other side was my name, Kristen Guillory, Ph.D. A few women told me that I needed to change my business card because it would intimidate men. They said my picture looked polished and fancy and that some men would be intimidated by my credentials. I kept my postcard as is.

I recall attending a conference about three months after I graduated with my Ph.D. During that conference, I attended a workshop and introduced myself as Dr. Kristen Guillory (look, y'all, I was going to take advantage of my new credentials). Another time, I remember being in the grocery store line and answering my phone by saying, "Dr. Guillory," knowing my mom was calling me. I just wanted people to know!

But back to the conference!

After the conference ended, an older African American woman approached me. I thought she was coming to congratulate me on my degree. Instead, she said, "You don't have to introduce yourself like that."

"What do you mean?" I asked.

She said, "You weren't born with 'doctor' in front of your name. You do not have to introduce yourself like that. Let people find that out."

While I was shocked by what she said, I replied, "Thank you for your input, but with all due respect, my mentor Dr. Shirley King told me to always address myself as such."

Her words saddened me. This was a woman who seemingly was in her late 60s, and I was 27 years old. She tried to dim my light. And if I did not have the encouragement from my mentor, I might have stopped addressing myself as Dr. Guillory.

During one of my speaker bootcamps, one of the participants approached me and said that she had been told her entire life that she was too much and too loud, so much so that she thought something might have been wrong with her. She wanted to tone herself down. I told her not to tone down who she is and, instead, to bless us with that energy and always shine. She was grateful for our conversation.

Another participant in another bootcamp informed me that during a job interview, she got feedback and was told that her lipstick was too bright. Yes, you read that correctly. She was told that her lipstick was too bright, which was the only feedback she got. After that, this brilliant, beautiful Black woman began to mute herself and tone down the colors she liked. She shared with me that she saw one of my headshots one day, a picture of me showing my shoulders, wearing my braids, and doing the Milly Rock dance, and she said that picture gave her so much freedom. After discussing additional details about how that feedback impacted her, I encouraged her to begin wearing bright colors again and be exactly who she is. She has done so ever since. Oh, she is out here blessing us with all the color!

Shortly after that conversation, I chatted with Kesha, a corporate real estate agent, invited to speak about diversity at an event for her job. She asked me to help her with her talk and key points. While we were working, she mentioned that she was on the step team in high school and stepped in college. She loved stepping! As we continued to talk, she said, "You know, I was peeping the scene in high school, looking for groups that I'd like to hang with." Because she said that with such ease, I knew it was the language she used when she was comfortable. So, I encouraged her to say "peeping the scene" in every talk she gave.

"Really?" she asked.

"Yes!" I exclaimed. "If that is authentically you, be you!" I said.

She also mentioned her love of a particular hip-hop song. And guess what? I encouraged her to incorporate that in her talks as well.

So, we created a talk that included stepping, "peeping the scene," hip-hop, her experiences, and her brilliance. As we were ending the conversation, she began to tear up and said, "I never knew I could incorporate all of me in any one area. Being a young Black woman, I have always hidden certain aspects about myself."

Whether we did not want to stand out, did not want people to think we were bragging, were told to tone down, did not fit into the work culture, or did not want to offend people, I would dare to say that most of us have dimmed our light. Well, no more! Bless us with your light! Your light is a light like none other. Do you realize that?

Take a moment to reflect on times you have dimmed your light. It might be too many to count. Maybe it has become the norm for you. Well, we are going to put a stop to that! Okay?

Look! No More Dimming Your Light

How have you dimmed your light?

_____

_____

_____

_____

_____

Why did you dim your light?

_____

_____

_____

_____

_____

What have you dimmed?

_____

_____

_____

_____

_____

Look, Stop Hiding!

If you have ever been told something like "you are too much," "you are too loud," or "you are too energetic," how did you respond?

___

___

___

___

What will it look like if you embrace who you are and do not care what others think of you?

___

___

___

___

Who would you be if you did not dim your light?

___

___

___

___

What is a step you can take this week to no longer dim your light?

_____

_____

_____

_____

_____

When will you take the step? Be specific. On what day? Put it in your calendar.

_____

Breaking Out of the Box

It was a warm fall afternoon, and I was walking on a college campus in some of my cute high heels (never under four inches), heading back to my office, when a student stopped me and asked, "Dr. Guillory, are you single?"

"Yes," I answered.

"Oh, good!" the student replied.

"Why good?" I asked.

"Because you're happy, and you wear heels," the student said and walked away.

I was so confused but later realized that seeing a single, happy woman was abnormal, not just to her but to many on campus. And the fact that I was wearing heels because I liked them and not to attract a man made me double weird. Over the course of that school year, I spoke to at least 100 women on the campus who never knew that being single was okay and even a blessing. Many students shared stories about feeling pressured to date and fit in certain boxes regarding relationships and timelines.

I remember leaving the campus gym, a student stopped me and said, "Dr. Guillory, my pastor told me to hurry up and get in a relationship so I can be engaged by the time I graduate." I was appalled. I could see the pressure on her shoulders. She looked so distraught.

I said, "I am so sorry he told you that. You do not have to be engaged before you graduate. You don't even have to date if you don't want to."

She looked at me with such relief.

***

Going to parties was the thing to do when I was in college.

What about you?

Look, I can remember my favorite party songs: "Back that Thang Up" by Juvenile, "Get it Ready" by DJ Jubilee, and "Drag Em Through the River" by UNLV (oh my goodness, that title and song lyrics – yikes!). During my first two years, I often went to parties and clubs, but my friends in college never knew that I never really enjoyed many aspects of parties and clubs. Many times, I did not really want to go. I did not like smelling like smoke or my ears ringing from the loud music. I did not like the aggressive men, either. Also, I did not want to talk to anyone when I was leaving the club. Back in my day, it was called "posting up." My goodness, I could not stand posting up! When it was time to go, I was ready to go. I did enjoy hanging with my friends and dancing. I enjoyed dancing by myself more than some stranger standing behind me. As I have reflected on that time, I realized that I went to parties and clubs because I thought that is what we are supposed to do. I did not think about the fact that I did not have to go, and I could have stepped out of that box.

What is something you have done because it was expected of you, but you really didn't like it or most aspects of it?

_____

_____

_____

In graduate school, on the first day of class, the professor often asks the students to introduce themselves and share a little something. During my Ph.D. studies, my classmates would say things like they wanted to be a professor or a researcher. When it was my turn, in a joking manner, I said, "I want to rule the world." Being a professor was never a long-term goal of mine. I knew I wanted to help and inspire people in different ways.

I taught my first college course at 24, and a few years after I graduated with my Ph.D., I became a professor. There was an open faculty position at a university in Texas. Two of my colleagues were already professors there. What they do not know is that they both texted me within 24 hours, informing me of this open position, and thought I would be great for it. I dismissed the first text because I was not interested. When I got the second text, I thought, "Okay, let me really think about this and consider it."

Well, I interviewed for the job and got it! Although being a professor was never my end goal, I enjoyed it and loved connecting with my students over the course of ten years.

I would teach in my own way, a very atypical method of teaching. We danced, rapped, role played, went out of the classroom, had poetry slams, created fake talk shows, and much more! I busted out of that traditional teaching box.

During a conversation with a woman working on her Ph.D. in social work, she told me that she did not want to go the traditional academic route. I asked her what she wanted to do. She hesitated and said, "What I want to do doesn't really fit with getting a Ph.D." I asked her to tell me anyway.

"I really want to write comic books," she said.

I said, "Oh, that's great! I can see you doing a lot with that."

"Really!?" she asked excitedly. "I have only told a few people about that dream because I thought I would be judged."

Right then, she broke out of the box.

Maybe it isn't a comic book for you, but what is something you would like to do that does not fit into "the box"?

_____

_____

_____

Sometimes it only takes one person to shame us into hiding our true passion and authentic self. When you have a dream or idea, be careful not to allow other people's opinions or comments to diminish your dream and goals. Strive to make yourself available for input that is uplifting and edifying. If someone has a negative opinion (I do not mean constructive) about your dream or goal, you can say something like, "I hear you. I'm excited about what is ahead and look forward to the future." And remember, you do not have to respond at all. You also do not have to make yourself available for unsolicited input. Protect that dream, protect your goals, protect your vision, protect your peace and protect your heart by any means necessary. I have had to do this on my journey, and it proved fruitful.

What can you do to protect your dreams, goals, vision, peace, and heart?

_____

_____

_____

How can you make yourself unavailable to input that is not uplifting or edifying?

_____

_____

_____

As a speaker, I am fully myself on stage – sharing humor, music, slang, and intellect, you name it, yet there are a few times I hid some of those elements because I thought it was too much. I thought people might not understand. There were times I tried to fit into the public speaking box, a box, quite frankly, that was boring, a box that was never meant for me. After becoming a speaker coach and developing various frameworks, I recognized that many public speaking frameworks were created a long time ago and not created with me in mind, a Black woman. These frameworks dismissed who I am and tried to box me in.

At the end of one of my speaker bootcamps, a group of women came up to me and said, "You demolished everything we thought a speaker was supposed to be! You are real and funny. You danced and went around to meet and talk to people, and you talked about your mistakes."

They were astonished.

They told me I gave them permission to be who they are.

When you think of what it means to come across as professional, what comes to mind? Maybe a certain type of attire, a certain way to speak, certain colors? Did you know that traditional professional boxes were not created with many of us in mind, either? Think about the fact that there are rules in place to manage the hair of Black people. Professionalism, for a long time, has only looked like one thing.

Well, guess what?

I am professional in my braids, my sweatshirt, and my humor. After working with so many who had tried to fit in boxes that were never created for them and seeing the negative impact, I wanted to help even more.

How are you breaking out of that professional box?

_____

_____

_____

A few years back, I reviewed a video of a talk from one of my clients, Micaela. During this video, she said a variation of "I am funny" three times in her talk. When I chatted with her, I said, "Your talk was good, but you told me you were funny three times but never made me laugh."

She said, "I think I've been in corporate America so long that I forgot to be me."

Fast forward, Micaela started to be herself and show up fully in her talks and on social media. At this point, she has over two million video views, and she is walking in freedom! Oh, and she started an entire social media branding and monetizing business.

A few months later, I reviewed April's video. She loves poetry and photography yet mentioned none of it in her talk. When she and I spoke about this, I said, "I wonder why you didn't implement any of you in this talk."

She said, "I think I've been in higher education so long, and as a young Black woman, we are told in so many ways that we need to fit into a certain box and hide who we are."

Since then, she has launched a photography series and a coaching program and is writing and sharing her poetry.

They broke out of the box.

***

Many of us have used the speaker persona when public speaking.

What is the speaker persona?

This is when you hit the stage and become the "professional speaker" you believe you are supposed to be—changing your voice, language, and posture, another version of you, if you will. I was once asked if the speaker persona could be a form of code-switching, and my answer was a resounding yes! Now, I'm not talking about getting into your zone and getting your Sasha Fierce on.

A *Harvard Business Review article* once mentioned the following:

Code-switching involves adjusting one's style of speech, appearance, behavior, and expression in ways that will optimize the comfort of others in exchange for fair treatment, quality service, and employment opportunities.[1]

The part that stands out to me is "optimize the comfort of others." Research has shown that code-switching can cause a psychological toll.[2] How often do we believe we must change who we are for the comfort of others while we experience discomfort? How often do you change to "optimize the comfort of others"?

For many, code-switching to fit into a box and make others comfortable has unfortunately become a norm that many do not realize they are implementing.

There is no judgment here.

---

[1] McCluney et al. 2019

[2] "This Survival Tactic Many BIPOC Use Could Be Harmful to Their Mental Health," n.d.

We must do what we have to do. For many, if code-switching did not occur, they may not be where they are, professionally speaking.

Shout out to you for making it this far.

Shout out to you for overcoming hurdles no one knows about.

Shout out to you for showing up in the best ways for yourself in various moments. I wonder if you can relate to me or any of the stories I shared in this chapter. I wonder if there were moments you were uncomfortable while trying to put yourself into a box. I wonder about the toll it has taken on you. Oh, but I have good news! You can break out of these boxes and break out of them in the best way for you that will protect your mind and heart. But whatever you do, it is time to break out of the box!

Let's dig a little deeper.

When have you code-switched? Who were you trying to make comfortable?

_____

_____

_____

In what boxes have you tried to fit?

_____

_____

_____

What has been the impact of trying to fit into a box that was never meant for you?

_____

_____

_____

What box do you need to break out of?

_____

_____

_____

What would it feel like for you to break out of the box?

_____

_____

_____

What is a step you can take this week to break out of that box? Maybe tell someone what it is, research something, post something on social media, say "no," or pursue that dream!

_____

_____

_____

When will you take the step? Be specific. On what day? Put it in your calendar.

_____

To Do

List 15 cool things about yourself (hobbies, experiences, accomplishments, favorites songs, talents, and so forth).

1. _____
2. _____
3. _____
4. _____
5. _____
6. _____
7. _____
8. _____
9. _____
10. _____
11. _____
12. _____
13. _____
14. _____
15. _____

BONUS: Share this list and a picture of yourself on social media. Use the caption "15 cool things about me! Which ones do we have in common?"

_____

_____

_____

_____

_____

_____

Their Understanding Is NOT Required... Okay?

I was on a weekend getaway with my best friend in May of 2014. Both mornings, as I sat on the balcony, I heard the Lord say, "It's time," and I quickly ignored that. You see, I knew what He meant, and I had no desire to leave my professor position. I was a great professor, and I had a great job. I liked steady money, and the idea of leaving was scary and unpredictable. All summer, the Lord continued to press upon my heart that it was time to leave that position. Well, I told the Lord that if I had a job lined up by July, I would leave. Yes, I sure did tell the Lord what I was going to do. Yet, I wanted to be obedient to the Lord, but I did not want that journey. In early July, I went to the Kids Across America camp with my sister and her family. She invited me to participate in Tree Tops, which is like a ropes course 30 feet in the air.

It was scary, y'all!

I have a fear of heights. I was afraid of falling, and I wanted to turn around, but we made it to the end!

The next morning, the Lord used that experience as an analogy for what would be my next journey. He revealed that, like the Tree Tops experience, I would want to turn around, be scared, and be afraid of falling, aka failing, yet He reminded me that I was protected in a harness and would not be harmed. He said, "In the same way you were in the harness, I will be with you and carry you on this journey."

Right then, I decided to leave my tenure track professor position.

When I returned from camp, I informed my department colleagues and ten other colleagues on campus about what I was doing. I told them that the Lord was leading me in a different direction. I told my colleagues that I would have to rely on the Lord like I had to rely on the harness from the Tree Tops experience. I told them that I knew the journey would be difficult, but I would not quit and knew I had to complete this new journey. I told them that I thought the Lord was leading me to pursue speaking in a full-time capacity. I also told friends and family of my decision to leave my professor position. I was excited and nervous. Frankly, I was fearful. I also knew I would have a lot of support from my university colleagues, friends, and family. Well, I received support but not at the level I anticipated.

I remember what people said to me after I told them about my plans. After I emailed my department colleagues about my decision with details from the Tree Tops experience, no one emailed me back. Not one person. So, I shared it with one colleague face to face. One of the program directors thought I was leaving just to leave, and another said, "So how's that motivational speaking going" in a very sarcastic manner. I remember being perplexed by the lack of support, especially since this was a Christian university. Another colleague told me that I was one of the shortest stints as a professor there. I know he believed me to be a flighty person.

After I left, I was deeply saddened that I did not hear from anyone on that campus, except for two people, for which I am grateful for them.

After I told one friend about my departure, she said, "So what are you going to do? Are you sure that's the best thing to do?"

I remember telling my dad, and I know he thought I was crazy. I told my mom, and I know she was not on board. Parents want their children taken care of, and they knew this would not be an easy journey.

Now about those who supported me from the jump – I told my best friend, who was incredibly supportive. I told another friend who said, "It's about time!" I also told my sister, aunt, and mentees, who were incredibly supportive. When I told the Vice President at that university about my decision, her response is something I will never forget. I went to her office to share the news, and I said, "I don't want you all thinking that I am flighty because I was only here for nine months."

She said, "Well, if we were blessed to have greatness for nine months, I would rather have that than nothing at all."

I was taken aback and honored by her words.

The first two years after leaving my job, I hid what I was doing because people would think I am crazy. I told people I was a professor. It was hard to let go of that title and the opinions of others. But I did, and I opened my hands to what the Lord had for me.

Since then, the more and more I have walked this journey and strived to move in obedience, the more I have not cared about what others think. Other people understanding how we move about the world is not required. Read that again. Other people understanding our purpose and destiny are not required. Other people agreeing with our journey is not required. As the quote says, "No one else is supposed to understand your calling. It wasn't a conference call."

My mom and dad came around and were incredibly happy for me, which was awesome but not required.

This is not the only time people did not understand or agree with my choices. The next one was my decision to travel abroad solo.

When I thought about my first extended solo international trip to Colombia, there was no doubt I would go, but I knew people were concerned and had questions. A few friends and family members were worried about my decision and expressed their concern. I had to reject their fear. I actually said that to one person, too. I said, "I have to reject your fear. Your fear has nothing to do with me. I am going to trust that the Lord will take care of me like He has all of these years."

Toward the end of my first solo trip, the same people that were worried were telling me that they wanted to travel to Colombia, too.

In 2021, I had a chat with a woman I have known for years, and she asked me about my speaking and coaching journey. She said she did not understand what led me to become a speaker coach and walk away from some of my other projects. I appreciated her asking me, but I also shared, "Respectfully, your understanding of my journey isn't required, but I'm so glad you asked instead of speculating."

People have the right to ask questions, and you have the right to answer or not answer. Be mindful only to make yourself available for statements and people that are uplifting, encouraging, and edifying.

Caring too much about the opinions of others affects how we make decisions, and, at times, many of us base our decisions on what others think or what we think they will think. Doing this leads to creating a life based on other people and not what we truly desire and are led to do. I know I do not want to have a life based on other people's expectations and opinions. And I am sure that is not the life you want.

Their Understanding Is NOT Required… Okay?

Is your life based on what you desire and are led to do or on other people? Maybe a combination of both.

_____

_____

_____

_____

Take a moment to reflect: Why did you choose your profession, college, to marry or remain single? Why have you waited so long to pursue that goal? The good news is that you can decide today to pursue a goal based on what you desire, based on where the Lord is leading you.

Share when you made a decision that many did not agree with or understand. What was the result?

_____

_____

_____

_____

Whose understanding and or approval have you been seeking but should surrender to the Lord?

_____

_____

_____

_____

Consider writing a letter to them. You do not have to give it to them, though. This will allow you to be no longer paralyzed due to seeking their understanding or approval. It is time to break free from the burden of needing the approval and understanding of others.

What dream, goal, or purpose do you have that you dim or water down out of fear that people will not understand?

_____

_____

_____

_____

Their Understanding Is NOT Required… Okay?

What dream, goal, or purpose have you not pursued out of fear of what others might say or think?

_____

_____

_____

Who is supportive of you?

_____

_____

_____

I encourage you to text them right now and thank them for their support.

What would it feel like if you moved in the direction you know you are supposed to move regardless of the understanding of others?

_____

_____

_____

What is a step you can take this week to move in that direction?

_____

_____

_____

When will you take the step? Be specific. On what day? Put it on your calendar.

_____

Over It!

Over the years, I have had hundreds of women reach out to me and share how grateful they were to see me on stage. Each time I hear this from other women, I feel honored. They have no idea how much they motivate me to continue.

After an engagement in Houston, Texas, in 2019, a woman came up to me in tears. She waited over 20 minutes to speak with me because others were asking me questions and thanking me for the presentation. I led an interactive training on how to have crucial conversations. I, of course, incorporated dancing (merengue), humor, and group work. The woman in tears said that she had never seen someone present the way I did. She said, "You came in here with your braids, with your personality, and you had us dancing, and you had this room of white people respecting you. I have never seen that. I've never seen a Black woman do that."

She went on to tell me that she is an attorney and sometimes downplays who she is. Actually, she hesitantly shared that she was an attorney. She was wearing a hat and said, "I have an afro and hide it sometimes." She also shared that she would often hide her personality, but with seeing me, she learned that one could command a room exactly as they are. She no longer wanted to apologize for her hair. She was over it!

After another talk, about six months later, I received a message from someone that said, "Five years ago, I was in your audience at my college, and the first thing you said was 'everybody, sit up straight.' I had never seen a Black woman present with so much authority and confidence." She told me I gave her permission to be herself. She noted that I did not apologize for being who I am, and she was over wanting to apologize for being herself.

Although I am in a place of being unapologetic, I have not always been this way. In the past, I apologized for asking questions, disagreeing with someone, and sharing facts about myself. Once, on a phone interview, I was asked to share my student evaluations for teaching. I said, "Not to brag, but I am rated as a top professor."

The interviewer said, "Now why did you say, 'not to brag?'"

Honestly, I had not thought about it. That statement, in a sense, was an apology for sharing facts about myself. I did not want to come across as thinking I was better than anyone. I was just stating facts which is never bragging.

But you know what?

We have the right to brag if we desire!

When have you added a statement like "not to brag" or apologized for stating facts about yourself?

_____

_____

_____

Now, write those items for which you once apologized. Write them as statements. (For example: I have a master's degree. I own a home. I travel. I have children, etc.)

_____

_____

_____

During a phone call with one of my clients, Brandi, she started talking about the many times she had been told to tone down and stop asking questions. She said, "You know, Dr. G, I am over apologizing for my energy. I am over being told I ask too many questions. I am over apologizing because I don't have enough degrees. I am over it."

Like Brandi, I am over it!

I've been over it –

Over dimming my light.

Over defending my choices.

Over apologizing for who I am.

Over men trying to tell women what to do with their intellect and bodies.

Over people placing their doubts on me.

Over being available for things that are not uplifting and edifying.

Over hiding my personality.

Over hiding my aggressive financial goals.

Over It!

Over hiding that I want to normalize Black women being millionaires.

Over giving energy to things and people that have nothing to do with me or my goals.

Over negative self-talk.

What about you? What are you over? What do you no longer want to apologize for? List below. Go all out!

I'm over _____

I'm over _____

I'm over _____

I'm over _____

I'm over _____

I'm over _____

I'm over _____

I'm over _____

I'm over _____

I'm over _____

I'm over _____

Now, say them out loud.

Powerful, right?

Now, select two of your "I'm over it" statements and list the first three steps to being over it (i.e., if you are over being told you are too much, step one could be to tell people you are not too much but just enough. Step two could be to commit to shining, and step three could be not to apologize to the next person who says that you are too much.)

I'm over:

_____

Step 1:

_____

Step 2:

_____

Step 3:

_____

***

Over It!

I'm over:

___

Step 1:

___

Step 2:

___

Step 3:

___

Time to Dream

When is the last time you dreamed?

I am not referring to your dreams at night. I'm asking about the last time you truly allowed yourself to dream, dream your heart's desires and your goals such as where you would like to live and vacation, your career, your mental health, your physical health, your spiritual health, your home, and your family. Have you really allowed yourself to go there?

I wonder if you have some dreams you never told anyone because you fear their response or think they will judge you.

Well, guess what?

You don't have to tell anyone.

I wonder if you have some dreams you have pushed to the side because you don't see how they might happen or think they are too big. As I often say, surrender the when and the how. You may not know when or how it will happen, but you know *what* you desire to happen. Lean into the dream.

They are your dreams.

There is a reason you desire to help the people you help in the way you do.

There is a reason you desire to visit those countries.

There is a reason you desire to be on that stage.

There is a reason you desire to be a millionaire.

There is a reason you dream of providing scholarships to seniors at your former high school.

There is a reason you desire to build a home.

I believe the Lord gives us desires and dreams and allows us to have them. I have had dreams that I never shared with others, and when they came to fruition, I was overcome with gratitude. The following are some of those dreams:

- I had a dream to speak at an event in a large ballroom-type space with multiple large screens behind me. In 2017, while walking in a venue, I was overwhelmed because it was the venue for which I had dreamed.

- I love being by the water and among fun and laid-back people. During my first extended-stay trip in Colombia, my Airbnb host (who became a friend) invited me to spend New Year's Eve at her brother's home. Well, I didn't know it was a mansion on the beach. Around midnight, we went to the roof of the home, and fireworks began. I became emotional because more than I could have asked for was taking place.

- I had a dream for my sister and me to start hanging out more and traveling together. In 2020, the group trip to Colombia I planned was canceled due to COVID-19. Around the same time the following year, we went on a sister's trip to Florida.

- I heard someone say that they wanted to set their life up like a vacation, which resonated with me. I began to pray about it and write my affirmation about living by the water, particularly the ocean. I had no clue how or when it would happen; I just had a strong desire for this. Before I knew it, things lined up for that to happen. Yaaas, living by the beach!

- I had a dream to take an improv class, but it was during a time my finances were not as great as I would have liked. One day, I came across a scholarship for an improv class. I applied and got it!

It is essential to allow myself to dream, allow myself not to limit the Lord, and be open to what He has for me. I found that once I allowed myself to dream and write those dreams down, plans and action began taking place (Habakkuk 2:2).

I have plenty more dreams – financial dreams, health dreams, the ability to help others' dreams, travel dreams, business dreams, faith dreams, and more!

There are benefits to dreaming. Dreaming increases your excitement. Dreaming helps you focus. Dreaming gives purpose to those things you consider to be mundane. There is a potential mindset shift. Imagine what it might be like to lean into your big dreams instead of leaning into things like "nothing will ever change" or "my life is horrible." Dreaming instills hope.

During a six-week series I hosted, one of the assignments was to dream. I encouraged the participants just to go there and dream. I then asked them to share a few of their dreams. One of the participants shared that she dreams of buying a home on a lot of land. And a few minutes later, she came back and said, "I want the home to be on the land I own. So, I guess that is another dream, to be a landowner."

Now it's your turn. I want you to take 20 minutes to write any and every dream you have in your journal, nonstop writing in your journal. Dream big! Do not limit yourself. Do not limit the Lord. This is a variation of an activity I learned from one of my coaches, Dr. Tracy Timberlake. Dream about your health, finances, relationships, locations, knowledge, thoughts, family, home, and faith. Pause and get to dreaming. And go!

List 20 of your dreams.

1. _____
2. _____
3. _____
4. _____
5. _____
6. _____
7. _____
8. _____
9. _____
10. _____
11. _____
12. _____
13. _____
14. _____
15. _____
16. _____
17. _____
18. _____
19. _____
20. _____

Now let's create some goals. "Dreams are not goals. Goals are the strategy" (Tracy Timberlake). According to a Harvard Business Study, only three percent of people write down goals.[3]

Solution-focused counseling[4] believes goals are the first steps, not end results. Select five dreams from your list and write five steps to reach each dream.

Dream #1:

1. _____
2. _____
3. _____
4. _____
5. _____

---

[3] "New Tech Seattle." n.d. Www.newtechseattle.com. https://www.newtechnorthwest.com/the-psychology-of-writing-down-goals/.
[4] Peter De Jong and Insoo Kim Berg. 2008. *Interview for Solutions*. Belmont Brooks/Cole.

Look, Stop Hiding!

Dream #2:

1. _____
2. _____
3. _____
4. _____
5. _____

Dream #3:

1. _____
2. _____
3. _____
4. _____
5. _____

Dream #4:

1. _____
2. _____
3. _____
4. _____
5. _____

Dream #5:

1. _____
2. _____
3. _____
4. _____
5. _____

Nice work! Now go back and revisit the first step of each of your dreams. Next to that step, write a deadline to take those first steps. Get to it!

What is your prayer for your dreams?

_____

_____

_____

_____

_____

Now let's turn your goals or dreams into affirmations. If you dream of being a best-selling author, you will write I, (YOUR NAME), am a best-selling author. If you have a dream to be more grateful, you will write I, (YOUR NAME), am grateful all the time.

I, _____

I, _____

I, _____

I, _____

I, _____

I, _____

I, _____

I, _____

I, _____

I, _____

I, _____

I, _____

I, _____

I, _____

I, _____

I, _____

Paralyzing Thoughts

I was the afternoon speaker for a student event in Dallas, Texas. NFL great Dion Sanders was the morning speaker. My friend and amazing speaker, Raul Magdeleno, was the lunch speaker, and I was the closing speaker. As I was walking into the venue, Raul said, "Oh, Dr. G, I was getting ready to leave, but I have to stay to see you!"

I was thinking, "Oh, no. You're going to make me nervous."

That afternoon, I led an interactive talk for about 45 minutes. Afterward, many of the staff and students came to thank me. When I finished speaking with them, I walked to my car, opened the door, and sat inside, but I could not start the car because I thought I did a horrible job with my talk. I sat in the car for three hours, thinking that I did too much, that Raul would not think it was good, and believed the school would never invite me again. I sat in my car so long that a security guard came out and asked if I was okay. I was paralyzed by thinking I did not do a great job.

I finally made it home, and my best friend was there. She asked me how it went and, I said, "I guess it was okay," and then I walked away and began to cry. My friend asked me what was wrong, and I told her. She said, "I bet you did a great job."

I went to my room, still feeling crappy, so much so that I texted a friend of mine who happens to be an Olympic gold medalist. I texted her to find out if she had ever lost at anything. She said, "Of course." I then asked her how she got over it. She said, "Remember that you have another chance and learn from what you did so that you don't do it again."

I guess her advice was not enough, because I called my aunt. I said, "My talk was horrible," and she said, "So what if it was. You'll have other opportunities." I had never considered the "so what if it was" notion. She tried to help me understand that some talks may not go well, and I will survive.

All three pieces of encouragement were needed – my BFF saying, "I bet you did great," my Olympic friend saying, "Learn from what you did so that you don't do it again," and then my aunt saying, "So what if it was. You'll have other opportunities." I later realized what made me think my talk was horrible:

1. Raul stayed. Look, y'all, he was considered the top Latinx speaker in the country at that time and him being in the space made me so nervous.
2. My uncle had passed away a few days prior, and I was overly sensitive to things.
3. I thought I did too much. Yep, that's it. I sat back and said to myself, "So, I think it wasn't good because I had too many activities." Yeah, that was it!

I held on to thinking that I would never be invited back to speak for that school district. I honestly did not want to talk to the director who invited me. I was embarrassed due to the belief that I did not do a good job. About six months later, the director called me. We had a great two-hour chat, like two girlfriends, and she invited me to be a featured speaker at a conference. I could not believe I had been stuck on my negative thoughts for so long.

Have you ever been there? If a thought has ever paralyzed you, the following are six things to consider:

1. Accept that you cannot change the past.

2. Be mindful of your thoughts, attitudes, and assumptions. As my sister said, "What are the thoughts about your thoughts?"
3. Ask yourself if your thoughts are based on the truth.
4. Say the thought out loud or write them down to weaken the toxicity of the thought.
5. Strive to forgive yourself and be gentle with yourself.
6. Pray for guidance, peace, and clarity.

Over the years, I have worked with some of the most brilliant and gifted people. A good percentage of them have struggled with self-defeating, self-limiting, and paralyzing thoughts. During the first chat with Leonard, an awesome gentleman who would become one of my clients, I asked him about his passion for helping youth and young adults. As he was sharing, he mentioned a story about a time he spoke to a class. Months later, he received a phone call from a mother of a young man in that class. This mother thanked Leo for all he did to inspire her son. As Leonard was sharing this story with me, I said, "That's your story. Have you ever thought about sharing it?" He was shocked and said he had never thought about it.

Later, he joined one of my coaching programs, and we began to work on developing his speaker fees. He was extremely nervous about charging. It made him uncomfortable. He did not see the value he was offering. I recall him being nervous about charging $300. He kept working. He kept believing. He started to see what he was doing was valuable. Leonard now has confidence because he recognizes the value that he brings. We had a chat about a year later, and he told me that he was starting to believe that his fee of $5,000 was not enough.

Okay, Leonard!

So, I told him to increase his fee.

During a coaching call for my clients, I remember telling each client to increase their fees. It was now Jeannette's turn to share her fee.

I said, "So, what is your fee, Jeannette?"

She said, "$5,000."

I said, "Okay, great!"

One month later, during a one-on-one coaching call, she said, "Dr. Guillory, I have something to tell you. I'm not charging $5,000. I just said that because you were fussing at us and telling everyone to increase their fees."

I was shocked!

Jeannette did not believe that anyone would pay her that.

Fast forward a few months. When she shared her fee with potential clients, she got it!

During the booking call role play with another group, a client said, "Dr. G, what if no one will pay me?"

My response was, "Then they won't."

Did you catch that?

Our beliefs are particularly important. They can stifle, paralyze, or propel us. When thinking about my prior speaking engagement and my thoughts that my talk was horrible, I just didn't have nor used tools to work through them. Jeannette and Leonard did not believe they deserved to be paid as speakers.

Oh, but today they do!

I am no longer paralyzed by defeating thoughts, and Leonard and Jeannette believe and know they can charge their worth.

So, what about you? What beliefs about yourself have paralyzed you?

_____

_____

_____

_____

What have these beliefs paralyzed you from doing?

_____

_____

_____

_____

Let's create your paralyzing thoughts toolkit.

Review the suggestions on page 72. You can use all, some, or none of them. What are five things you can do when a thought paralyzes you?

1. _____
2. _____
3. _____
4. _____
5. _____

Now take a picture of this, so you have it on your phone when a thought tries to stop you!

What area of your life do you have trouble finding value?

_____

_____

_____

_____

What makes you valuable in that area?

_____

_____

_____

_____

Affirmations: I want you to create five affirmations about your value and beliefs in yourself or where you would like to be. For example:

I, Kristen, am financially free.

I, Kristen, am open to all the Lord has for me.

I, Kristen, give freely.

Paralyzing Thoughts

I, Kristen, offer immense value to every group I meet.

I, Kristen, learn from hurdles and setbacks.

1. _____
2. _____
3. _____
4. _____
5. _____

To Do

I challenge you to write ten affirmations every morning. Yes, the same affirmations. Feel free to use the ones you just created and your affirmations from "Time to Dream." You may not believe them yet but writing them every day is extremely helpful. Also, anytime you have a negative or toxic thought, I want you to write it down, say it out loud, or record yourself saying it. As Dr. Caroline Leaf would say, "We want to weaken the toxicity of thoughts." Y'all get that? We want to weaken the impact of the thought. I wonder what might have happened if I talked out loud and wrote what was on my mind when I sat in my car that day. Instead of doing that, I allowed the thoughts to swirl around in my head and get bigger and bigger, and they became toxic.

But no more!

Yaaas! You Better Show Up

I was invited to speak to NASA, y'all!

Yep, NASA.

It was an event hosted by Ford. When I arrived, I noticed the stage. It was lovely. The podium was in the middle, but there's only one thing – I don't like to use podiums when I speak. I sat at the banquet table and contemplated whether I would use a podium or ask if I could move it. I wanted to honor the space and honor myself. So, I figured the worst they could say is no. I made the request, and they said, "Absolutely. Please let us know if there is anything else you need."

I then thought, "Well, I'm going to keep my talk as is and reference the Yung Joc song as a part of my Ph.D. story."

Oh, we had a good time!

I even brought a woman on stage who did the Yung Joc motorcycle dance with me, and what was cool is that no one after me returned the podium to its original spot. Everyone after me seemed much more relaxed.

Look, Stop Hiding!

I was invited to speak at a university during a large chapel service where at least 1,000 students would attend. I already knew this university didn't play music with words too often, and I thought, "Well, what do I have to lose? I'm going to ask if I can play a hip-hop song." I asked, and the response was, "How long would you like us to play it?"

I thought, "Awww, snap!"

I arrived at the venue and recruited a few students to dance with me as I played "Uno Seis" by Andy Mineo and Lecrae. Half of the audience was feeling it and the other half looked a little confused. You see, I believe I was the first person to play a hip-hop song during chapel. It was not the norm, but there is nothing normal about me.

There was a woman I mentored who had a speaking engagement. The content was great. Her slides were fabulous. I only encouraged her to do one thing – add a line from a Beyonce song to the end of her talk. While her content was great, she did not allow us to get to know her at all. I did not want her to sing but reference a song by her favorite singer and connect it to her workshop. She pushed back on this suggestion for a good 15 minutes. "Dr. G, I try to keep that separate."

I told her, "I get that, but people connect to real and authentic."

After some encouragement, she decided to do it.

The next day, I received a text from her that read, "My talk went well. People loved it. I'm glad I listened to you. Thank you, my speaker coach!"

Yo is another fabulous client with the most beautiful energy and joy. She had thought that her energy was too much. I told her it was a gift from the Lord. One day, we had a chat. She told me about an upcoming call with podcast hosts in another country. She was worried about showing all her energy. I encouraged her to show up as herself. Her energy is contagious. That is why people want to be around her. After the podcast, she told me what a great time she had and that the main thing mentioned about her was her energy.

You show up for so many people. Don't you think it is time to show up for yourself? Maybe you were made to feel ashamed of who you are, or maybe there is some part of your past you are not proud of.

But guess what?

Your past does not define who you are. Other people's opinions of you do not define who you are. Frankly, their opinions are none of your business. It's time to show up. Show up in the way you want to show up. Show up by using your voice, setting boundaries, saying no by strutting your stuff, celebrating, showing your personality, singing, going on that trip, starting that business, taking that nap, and pursuing that goal. Whatever it is, you have got to show up. And remember, if your light is too bright, they can put on sunglasses!

Yaaas! You Better Show Up

What is a way you would like to show up?

_____

_____

_____

_____

_____

What if you show up as you are? What would that look like?

_____

_____

_____

_____

_____

What would that feel like?

_____

_____

_____

_____

_____

Look, Stop Hiding!

What are the benefits of showing up?

_____

_____

_____

_____

_____

What are the consequences?

_____

_____

_____

_____

_____

What does walking in freedom look like to you?

_____

_____

_____

_____

_____

A part of showing up is honoring our gifts and talents, and for too long, I did not do that. I often hear that I am an answered prayer. Many have told me that I am truly walking in my purpose and have helped them more than I know. I normally tell them that I received what they shared and feel honored, which is the truth. Years ago, I did not always receive words like that or "thank yous." I took them for granted.

In the Fall of 2015, I was reading through feedback at the end of an event where I was the keynote speaker. I was looking for a quote to add to my website. Every piece of feedback expressed gratitude, told me how they were transformed, how my energy is contagious, that I was walking in my gift, or did not expect what they received.

At that moment, I realized I had taken my gift for granted.

I had never really honored it.

I never really thought of my abilities and gifts as exceptional, which they are!

Today, as I show up, I strive to receive all the gratitude that comes.

Look, Stop Hiding!

What gifts have you taken for granted?

_____

_____

_____

_____

_____

How can you honor those gifts today?

_____

_____

_____

_____

_____

It's Time to Shine and Find Your Voice

It's time!

It has been long enough that you have not walked in the freedom of who you are.

It's been long enough that you have downplayed your voice.

It's been long enough that you have said yes to everyone but yourself.

I know you have had dreams and desires to do a bit more than what you are doing now, whether professionally, personally, for your mental health, physical health, or family, but something or someone has stopped you.

No more!

It's time! You have been waiting for far too long!

If you have ever worried about what people are going to say, think about a few things:

1. Who exactly are people? Think about the fact that you are still here despite "people" saying something.

2. Real talk, "people" are not thinking about you as much as you think. "People" have their own stuff to tend to.

3. Let's stop giving so much energy to people who take away from who you are. Instead, pour that energy into walking in the freedom of who you are, of who the Lord created you to be, pursuing your dreams and goals. How about pouring that energy into the people who support you, people who want to work with you? I do not know when it started, but way too much energy is spent talking about haters, people who do not like us, shady people, and people who do not support us. By the time we get to the end of dedicating our energy to this, we do not have the energy to do the things that give us life! Let's not give these too much time and energy. Really, take a moment to reflect on how much time you dedicate to these things. No more! If it does not have anything to do with your calling, dreams, or goals, stop giving it so much attention.

Do you know that you have the right to be heard? Do you know that your voice matters? Do you know that your voice is valuable? Do you know you have a powerful voice? Having a powerful voice does not mean that you are loud (I mean, I can be loud), but it means you know that your voice is powerful, you know when to use it, and you choose when to use it for the best of the situation. You have the right to do the following:

- Ask a question
- Say no
- Not downplay your credentials and talent
- Be silent
- Own your story
- Use your voice to ask for help
- Use your voice to say you are powerful and amazing
- Use your voice to Speak Life over yourself and other people
- Use your voice as a powerful tool
- Speak up for others
- Let your opinion be known
- Celebrate wins
- To laugh
- Compliment other people

- Say "thank you."

If needed, find your voice again! You have been silenced over the years. Maybe somebody or too many people told you to be quiet, you should be seen and not heard, or that your voice does not matter, or maybe you have thought that, but let me tell you right now that you need to be heard and you deserve to be heard.

It's Time to Shine and Find Your Voice

Let's make a promise to yourself. This is my promise to me regarding my voice:

_____

_____

_____

_____

My promise to myself regarding shining is:

_____

_____

_____

_____

My promise to myself regarding walking in freedom is:

_____

_____

_____

_____

Bonus: Visit www.futureme.org and write a note of encouragement to your future self in six months and 12 months.

I Recognize!

I designed the "I Recognize" statement to help people frame their messages and passion. I would like for you to create your own statement, but I am going to remix it, as I want you to create your personal statement for shining by writing the following:

- Blank 1: Your name.

- Blank 2: The problem you want to address pertaining to shining or your voice.

- Blank 3: Why is this a problem?

- Blank 4: Write the solution to the problem.

Fill in the blanks:

I, (your name) _____, recognize that I have dealt with/struggled with/hidden/am over (the problem) _____
for far too long due to (reason) _____
I am passionate about (the reason/the solution)

_____
_____

Example:

I, Jennifer, recognize that I have hidden my gifts for far too long due to being told that I was too much due to not wanting people to think I was bragging. I am passionate about shining and no longer hiding my accomplishments.

I challenge you to post that on social media or share it with one person you trust. I also encourage you to take a picture of it and put it somewhere to see it each day.

How will you do what you said you are passionate about?

_____

_____

_____

_____

How will you no longer hide your accomplishments and shine?

_____

_____

_____

_____

I Recognize!

Create three ways to execute your passion items:

1. _____
2. _____
3. _____

It is time, time to shine!

It's time to walk in the freedom and beauty of who you are with no apologies and no worries about what others think!

It's time to walk in the fullness of who the Lord created you to be.

It's time to pray for ease on your journey.

Have you ever prayed for ease?

I remember being asked to do this, and I thought it was crazy.

Do you go into things expecting to struggle?

Are you expecting this journey to be hard?

Do you think showing up will be hard?

Do you expect things always to be hard?

Do things sometimes happen easily, but you reject the ease?

I wonder if things easily happen for and to us, but we make it more difficult. For example:

- I wonder if this journey of never dimming your light again might be easier than you think.
- A relationship is going well, no drama, but you are waiting for the other shoe to drop and do not enjoy the good moments as much as you could.
- That difficult co-worker is being kind, but you know something is up.
- You apply for a job, the interview goes well, and you get the job with your requested pay. You think, "That was too easy. What's the catch?"
- You are buying a home, and the process is too easy or smooth, and you think something must be wrong.

Why lean into difficulty and believe that something will go wrong rather than leaning into ease? What about the things you are easily able to do? Maybe you don't see it as easy. Maybe you have the gift or anointing of ease in some areas. For me, it is almost like I was expecting things always to be difficult or challenging. I did not even realize this.

I do not want to live there. What about you?

I Recognize!

Well, I no longer do.

Yes, of course, use wisdom and discernment.

I am not saying we won't experience hardships. I know I have experienced my share, but do you expect everything to be hard? Trials develop perseverance (James 1:2-3), but the Word does not say trials will happen every minute of every day.

Yes, I pray for ease and include ease in my affirmations: I, Kristen, do things with ease, and things easily come to me.

I challenge you to pray for ease. Write your prayer for ease.

_____

_____

_____

_____

_____

While I pray for and lean into ease, this journey of walking in freedom, using my voice, and never dimming my light was not easy initially, but I wonder if it could have been.

Oh, but today!

I have grown a lot and continue to grow, but I can tell you that I feel more powerful and at peace every time I shine my light and walk in freedom. Walking in freedom is so important to my mental health. The more freedom I walk in, the more I can truly do what I have been called to do with no apologies.

I think about the years I downplayed who I was, hid who I was, tried to fit into a box, and downplayed who the Lord made me to be. I hid the gifts He gave me, and I tried to fit Him into a box.

No more!

And no more for you either!

In the words of Beyonce, "You ready? Let's go get 'em!"

The Dangers of Not Letting Your Light Shine

I hope you are ready to shine your light!

The world needs your light!

You are so very gifted as who you are *right now!*

Now, just in case you have some hesitation, that is okay. Please take the steps that work for you and allow yourself to be gentle with yourself. Here is an example of a step: I was chatting with a gentleman who works in corporate America who shared that he despises the dull colors and overall feeling in corporate America. He shared that he likes bright colors, and his favorite color is pink, but he was afraid to show this side of himself. I asked him if he would consider wearing pink socks to work. He thought this was a great idea.

So, what would be your pink sock moment?

Remember that shining does not mean that everyone can see what you are doing or who you are, but *you* know you are authentically you!

What is a pink sock moment for you?

_____

_____

_____

Did you know there are dangers of not letting your light shine? The following dangers could happen! They have been developed through the framework of my clients' experiences, research, my background in mental health, being a therapist for over four years, and personal experiences.

1. Toxic thoughts: Earlier in the book, I mentioned toxic thoughts. Toxic thoughts are negative thoughts that come from adopting the negative opinions of others, negative self-talk, and self-defeating thoughts. If you do not address these thoughts by journaling, counseling, or talking about them aloud to the Lord or a trusted friend, they will grow into potentially harmful outcomes. If you believe that you are not enough or your story is not valuable, imagine how that thought can grow and how it might manifest itself.

2. Mental health burden: Hiding who you are is extremely taxing on your mental health. You are essentially going against everything your mind is telling you to do and be.

Yet, you box yourself in to fit in. If you have ever code-switched and did it all day, you probably found yourself tired after work, wanting to lounge at the end of the day. Why is this? Because you have had to exert more energy all day long. Nothing is wrong with you. You are exhausted from trying to be someone you are not. Imagine the toll on your mental and physical health if this has taken place for years. Remember, nothing is wrong with you. You are exhausted. You need rest. You need support. You need to walk in freedom.

3. Forgetting about yourself: Your life might become one where you want to please others and forget about yourself. You could look up one day and say, "What am I doing? Why am I doing this? Who am I? You might look up one day and discover that you have created a life based on the expectations of others.

4. Resentment: You could become resentful of others living in their authentic glory. Resentment could lead to anger, frustration, sadness, and regret. Would you want to live in that place?

5. Lack of joy: You might experience a lack of joy or happiness and, in extreme cases, depression. Please seek counseling if this is you.

6. Tension: Tension could arise, the tension between who you really are and want to be and the person you think

you think you must be due to code-switching, not wanting to stand out, and not wanting others to think negatively about your choices. This tension could impact every aspect of your life. This tension leads to a lack of peace. You might have times when you are uncomfortable or unhappy, which could be due to this tension.

7. You will live with regrets. Many of us have regrets, but you do not want to regret not shining your light and walking in complete freedom. Regret leads to an emotional toll.

8. If you are a parent or aunt/uncle, you will be an example of someone who did not pursue your dreams and catered your life to the thoughts and opinions of others. And this will be passed on to them. Remember, children do what they see, not necessarily what they are told. So, what are your children, nieces, nephews, godchildren seeing you do in terms of shining your light?

9. You might turn to unhealthy habits to cope with the negative feelings associated with hiding yourself. Please seek help if this is you.

10. All those talents and gifts will go to waste. You were given your personality for a reason. You were given those gifts, talents, and desires for a reason.

These dangers are real. Maybe you have already experienced some of them. Please seek support if needed.

Now, let's talk about the benefits of never dimming your light are limitless. Note - *the benefits are not guaranteed, and you must commit to doing the consistent work to show up and never dim your light.* Here are my top 12:

1. You will walk in freedom. Freedom! Sit in that for a minute. What would that feel like? How would that be for you?

2. Your light will rub off on others. It is truly a domino effect. You will give your friends, children, clients, and community permission to show up and shine!

3. You will experience increased joy and happiness. How are your joy and happiness these days? It will increase as you do the work to shine!

4. You will experience increased productivity because you are not using additional energy to hide your true self. Imagine that! What if you were able to be 10% more productive? What would you do? What about 20% more productive?

5. You will not care as much about the opinions of others because you will know that you are where you are supposed to be. When you are clear on who you

are, not too many things will make you waver. How would that feel to no longer care what other people think?

6. Your overall mental health will improve. Come on, mental health! Mental exhaustion is far more taxing than physical exhaustion. Your mental health is important and should be a priority!

7. Things that once bothered you won't bother you anymore. Come on, somebody!

8. Things will happen with ease. Come on, ease! Be sure to be open to all of it.

9. More opportunities could present themselves because you are more open.

10. You will feel more relaxed.

11. You will experience more peace.

12. You will experience all that the Lord has for you.

Let's walk that walk! *So, is it worth it to never dim your light again?*

41 Not-So-Typical Speaker Tips

But wait, there's more! I can't write a book about finding your voice and never dimming your light and not leave you with some golden public speaking nuggets.

Traditional speaker frameworks have dismissed the essence of people of color, particularly Black women and other women of color. We have dismissed our essence on stage because it may not fit. Well, we are *not* trying to fit in, okay? Too often, those who do any type of public speaking have adopted a particular speaker persona which is a form of code-switching, as mentioned earlier in the book. Below are 41 things I do as a speaker. Check them out!

1. *Be you*: Yes, you! No need to try to be anyone else when you are on that in-person or virtual stage.

2. *Cultivate relationships*: I strive to cultivate relationships, meaning if someone wants to book me to speak, I'm not just talking to them about the engagement. I'm talking to them about themselves and what they do. I can't tell you how many conversations have gone to the left while talking about traveling or my love for my nephews. Instead, I am doing life.

3. *Do well with what you have*: I do not have many social media followers compared to other speakers and coaches. I do well with what I have. There was a time I thought I needed more followers to do what I do. But that changed when a colleague, who did not have many followers, was consistently booking. I saw him on stage, and he knocked it out of the park; people really connected with him. I have had clients who have 200k, 300k, and 400k+ followers. They were pursuing speaking, but I have had more opportunities and paid more. Why? Because I know I am a speaker. I was consistent in posting and using what I had. They were not consistent, and people did not know that they were pursuing speaking.

4. *Do people know that this is what you are striving to do*: Be sure your support system is aware you are a speaker or desire to be one. If I look at your social media pages, do I know you give talks or trainings?

5. *I invest in coaching*: What is interesting is that I did not start investing in coaching until well into my professional speaking career and had experienced some success. I did not realize I needed coaching, and I kind of thought I knew everything. While I love being a coach, I will never not have a coach.

6. *I hear the need when I am on the booking call*: There is a process I use. This is a process with intentional steps. I hear the heart. I hear what is needed.

7. *I know my content*: If things shift a bit, it doesn't take me off my game because if I am leading a workshop and tell that we need to stay in a particular area for a minute, I can do so. Sense the heart of the need and heart of the audience.

8. *I write my outlines*: I go over and over and over the topic, even if it is the same talk. Even though I have spoken over 1,000 times, I still practice.

9. *I push myself to try new things in my talks.*

10. *I don't ever need to be comfortable*: Comfortable is not good. Comfortable is the enemy of greatness and excellence because I get too complacent. When I am comfortable, I lean on myself too much.

11. *I tell you to do something immediately in my tips and strategy*: I encourage people to do something now. People really appreciate this. For example: If you are leading a women's empowerment talk, say, "What I want you to do right now is (fill in this blank)."

12. *I create an experience*: Part of my experience is music, movement (i.e., dancing), connecting with other people, and audience interaction.

13. *I am me*: Humor, music, colorful braids, slang, and more.

14. *I know I am good at what I do*: You need to know this.

15. *I accept thank yous*: There was a time when I did not truly accept the "thank yous" and appreciation I received after speaking engagements. I dismissed them because I focused on what I thought did not go well, or I dismissed them because I did not recognize my gift.

16. *I know I can always grow and learn.*

17. *I use and honor my God-given gifts*: We all do. I strive to use them well. I took my God-given gifts for granted. No more. I honor and cultivate them.

18. *I use my experience as a professor, youth minister, and therapist.*

19. *90% of my opportunities have come from word of mouth.* I strive to knock it out on stage, which leads to other invitations.

20. *My talks create other opportunities.*

21. *I have booked opportunities from sharing a bit about me in conversations.* I am not always looking to close the deal. I strive to do life with people.

22. *I know my story is valuable.*

23. *I do not hide my light*: People do not know how brilliant you are until you show them.

24. *I am interactive*: Always interactive.

25. *At the end of my talks, I have offered myself as support if the person did not have anyone.*

26. *My follow-up game is strong*: I follow up after opportunities. A lack of a follow-up is one of the main opportunities for growth for speakers.

27. *I create opportunities*: It is an honor to get on other stages, and I create my own.

28. *I do not wait for things to come or fall in my lap*: I reach out to clients I already know. I also create stages to create opportunities.

29. *I am in it for the long haul*: You may connect with the client, and they may not be able to bring you in now but keep doing life with them. For example: I connected with a company three years ago, and the first thing I did was support one of their employee resource groups.

30. *I have strategically offered my talks for free*: A client asked me to lead a webinar for free. It was for 200 people. I decided to do it for exposure and connections. After that, I was invited to keynote one of their events. Then I was invited to lead a series for women and speak at a national event. I was compensated for these, and it all began from agreeing to speak for free.

31. *I do not give up*: I have seen too many give up after six months or one year. I have seen people give up after three months. Don't do that.

32. *I do not chase the money*: Money is not #1, but I get my coins.

33. *I strive to give*: I use discernment and wisdom, and if I am led to donate my talk, I do. If I believe that I need to offer more, I do so.

34. *I strive to over-deliver.*

35. *I have champions*: It is important to have champions. You have got to have people who champion you and know that you are good at what you do, people who can speak for you at those tables before you are in the decision-making chair. Many champions of mine had spoken up for me and pushed for me when people did not want me to be there.

36. *I am consistent*: You must be consistent in your voice, work, and on social media.

37. *Do not chase the contracts*: I had just given a keynote speech and received a standing ovation. Afterward, I was signing my books, but I was so focused on trying to get a contract with this company that, at one point, I ignored the 70 people in line who wanted to meet me. I saw them, but I was not present because I wanted a contract and another opportunity.

38. *I strive to learn from my mistakes*: Look at them as opportunities for growth.

39. *I do not review feedback within 48 hours of a talk*. I am extremely hard on myself. Any bit of feedback, I will catastrophize, which isn't good. I also want to be present for the people who are there. Waiting at least 48 hours allows me to be in a better space to receive and read the feedback.

40. *I strive to be gentle with myself.*

41. *I pray.*

What tips stood out to you, and how will you implement them?

Let's stay connected!

 @Dr. Kristen Guillory

 @Drkristenguillory

 Drg@kristenguillory.com

 www.kristenguillory.com

Made in the USA
Columbia, SC
02 March 2023

13094392R00072